TRIUMPH OF THE TRUTH

BOOKS FROM CLEMENS & BLAIR
— www.clemensandblair.com —

The Book of the Shulchan Aruch, by Erich Bischoff
For My Legionnaires, by Corneliu Codreanu
Myth and Sun, by Martin Friedrich
Unmasking Anne Frank, by Ikuo Suzuki
Pan-Judah! Political Cartoons of Der Stürmer, by Robert Penman
Passovers of Blood, by Ariel Toaff
The Poisonous Mushroom, by Ernst Hiemer
On the Jews and Their Lies, by Martin Luther
Mein Kampf, by Adolf Hitler
Mein Kampf (Dual English-German edition), by Adolf Hitler
The Essential Mein Kampf, by Adolf Hitler
The Myth of the 20th Century, by Alfred Rosenberg

BOOKS BY THOMAS DALTON
— www.thomasdaltonphd.com —

The Steep Climb: Essays on the Jewish Question
Classic Essays on the Jewish Question: 1850 to 1945
Debating the Holocaust
The Holocaust: An Introduction
The Jewish Hand in the World Wars
Eternal Strangers: Critical Views of Jews and Judaism
Hitler on the Jews
Goebbels on the Jews
Streicher, Rosenberg, and the Jews: The Nuremberg Transcripts

TRIUMPH OF THE TRUTH

by
Robert Penman

Clemens & Blair, LLC
— 2023 —

CLEMENS & BLAIR, LLC

Copyright © 2023, by Robert Penman
Chief Editor: Thomas Dalton, PhD

All rights reserved. No part of this publication may be reproduced, stored in a retrieval system, or transmitted, in any form or by any means, electronic, mechanical, photocopying, recording, or otherwise.

Clemens & Blair, LLC, is a non-profit educational publisher.
www.clemensandblair.com

Library of Congress Cataloging-in-Publication Data

Penman, Robert
Triumph of the Truth

p. cm.
Includes bibliographical references

ISBN 979-8987-7263-03
(pbk.: alk. paper)

1. World War Two
2. History, Germany
3. Jewish Question, the

Printing number: 9 8 7 6 5 4 3 2 1

Printed in the United States of America on acid-free paper.

Contents

Publisher's Introduction	1
A Personal Appeal	5
The Jewish Origin of Communism	8
Zionism: The Other Arm of Jewish World Domination	15
The Balfour Declaration	16
Hitler Comes to Power	19
The Second World War	27
What About "the Holocaust"?	34
War's End, and Post-War	38
Criticize the Jews? Never!	47
Looking Ahead	51
Recommended Books and Videos	56
Appendix A: Assorted Graphics and Memes	59
Appendix B: Original Cartoons by Robert Penman	67
Endnotes	75

TRIUMPH OF THE TRUTH

Publisher's Introduction

World War Two ended nearly 80 years ago. So much has changed in the world since then, and yet, much is the same. On the one hand, the war can seem like ancient history—a time before one's parents or grandparents were even born. For many, it might as well be 800 years ago.

And yet: why do we still hear so much about it? Why do references to the war, to Hitler, to the Nazis, and to the Holocaust still show up, constantly, in the popular media? Scarcely a day goes by without someone in the mass media slandering someone as a Nazi, or condemning some reference to Hitler, or invoking the Holocaust in some way. Why do these things never leave us?

There are good reasons for this, and they explain much about how the world works today. The same forces that dredge up constant references to Nazis are also able to dictate other aspects of what you see and hear in the media. They can dictate the kinds of movies you watch, the kind of music you listen to, and much about the kind of culture you have. To do this, these forces must have a large amount of wealth and vast political connections at their disposal. Consequently, they are also able to steer events at the highest levels. Why is there inflation? Why are we having a recession? Why did the housing market collapse? Why did the crypto market go south? Why are our politicians so incompetent and corrupt? Why is there a war in the Ukraine? All these questions are related.

In this short booklet, the artist and writer Robert Penman points to an answer. He relates his personal story of a quest for answers and of finding solutions. Here, in a most condensed and compact form, he offers an outline of the world that you will never find elsewhere. As it turns out, there is both "history that we read in school" and then "history as it actually happened," and these are not the same things. Countless inconvenient facts somehow never make it into school textbooks. Countless facts never appear in films or documentaries. Countless vital details are somehow left out of all discussions of Hitler, the Nazis, or the war. And these details make all the difference.

Obviously, such a small book can only be a start. Penman does an exceptional job of raising the right questions and citing the real sources behind events, but all this is only a beginning. The reader is invited to explore on his own—to confirm what is stated here, and to dive deeper into the relevant aspects of the past. At the end of this book, the reader is pointed to further resources to help him pursue his own quest for the truth.

All this is not mere history. It is *history that matters*. It is history that still exists, and still lives today. It is history that has a grave relevance to our collective future. This book comes not a moment too soon.

> *"There will come a day when all the lies will collapse under their own weight, and truth will again triumph."*
> — Dr. Joseph Goebbels

"There will come a day, when all the lies will collapse under their own weight, and truth will again triumph"
Dr Joseph Goebbels
May 1945

TRIUMPH OF THE TRUTH

A Personal Appeal

In late 2018, for whatever reason—probably because of my interest in history and a need to understand why this world is the way it is—I stumbled upon a view of recent world history that I hitherto had only heard hints of. I am careful when examining new information, and I know that the Internet has given voice to every bizarre type of theory and thought.

However, when I found links to sites from reputable researchers and historians, backed with a large amount of primary evidence, and regarding subjects most of us thought we knew, I was intrigued. The story they gave was very different from what I learned in school and through the media.

The subjects in question were:

- The origins of communism
- Capitalism and international banking
- Zionism
- Jewish influence on the above three issues
- Adolf Hitler
- National Socialism (the "Nazis")
- Germany
- The First & Second World Wars
- Winston Churchill
- Joseph Stalin
- Franklin D. Roosevelt
- The "Holocaust"
- Control of Hollywood and mainstream media

The things I found out from these historians, researchers, and documentary makers were such a shock! I could scarcely believe what I saw. It seemed that almost everything we have been led to believe about The Second World War, Hitler, National Socialism, and so on was wrong: distorted, edited, censored, or even outright lies. And most of it could be proven so! Honestly, I was devastated, heartbroken, and angry. I went through sleepless nights trying to come to terms with it all. Eventually I came to understand both the truth of things, and how the false ideas came to dominate society. It took some time and a lot of effort, but I did it.

Despite the difficulties, I would go through it all again, to know what I know now. The benefits have been tremendous. Many things that I previously found confusing or strange now fall into place. I still have lots of questions, but things make a lot more sense. I understand better how things work at the highest levels, and I have good idea about why certain things happen (or don't happen!) today. It has been a huge advantage for me, simply to have a better, more accurate picture of history and the world today.

Maybe all this sounds like some crazy 'conspiracy theory'; I hope not. All I ask is that you look into things yourself, become aware of some basic facts, and take the time to think about things in an open way.

This small booklet is just a start. Here, I want to give readers a basic overview of what I have learned, and provide some basic facts to help people think more clearly. There is not much text here—mostly graphics, photos, cartoons, and other visual aids. But the quotations and the facts here have been carefully checked and confirmed; there is nothing worse than putting out false or misleading information on these subjects!

I also realize that many readers will want more information than I provide here. At the end, I have included a "suggested reading" list for those who want to go into more details on these issues. You might not realize it yet, but even getting a good reading list is a very tough challenge these days! There is so much confusion, bias, and misinformation out there that a person could waste months or years chasing down false leads. Here, I have given the reader the best resources, in order to benefit from my own years of reading and research.

But above all, I urge you to persevere! We desperately need people to grasp the truth. In the end, the truth will triumph.

*****

What follows are some key points to historical events from the 20th century through to today. I present this via *infographics* that I have created. Infographics can be any kind of picture, usually accompanied by a bit of text—a photo, a drawing, a cartoon, a collage. Infographics offer a concise method for key facts to be shown and to be remembered by the reader. Below each graphic, or in the endnotes, I include the source information, for those who are interested.

Much of what is presented here will come as a shock to most people, from whom this history has been hidden. But it is true nonetheless, as we can confirm. Please read this with an open mind, and you will certainly learn much from it.

The Jewish Origins of Communism

What, exactly, is 'communism,' and where did it come from? Most people today believe communism to be simply a political movement (though terribly flawed), one that grew from intellectuals whose motive was to create a fairer world with equality for all. Yet, few know of its true origins, and that it was Jewish at its core.

The father of modern communism was a German Jew, Karl Marx, who lived from 1818 to 1883. In 1848, at the age of 30, he and Friedrich Engels published a small pamphlet called *The Communist Manifesto*. There, he outlined his basic principles of communism:

- All social conflict is due to *class struggle*—between the rich (the 'bourgeoisie') and the working class (the 'proletariat').
- The rich gain their wealth by exploiting the workers.
- The only way to fix this situation is by "forcible overthrow of all existing social conditions"—which means, violent revolution!
- The revolution must be global; all workers everywhere need to revolt against their upper classes.
- A new communist world will have no private property, no rich, no poor, no 'classes' at all. Everyone will be free and equal.

But this, of course, would mean massive amounts of bloodshed and warfare. The rich will not give up their wealth easily! Therefore, said Marx, we need to *take it by force*.

Here is what one recent Russian commentator had to say:

> "To understand the Jewish connection to communism, it may be helpful to start at the beginning—with Karl Marx and his lesser-known mentor, Moses Hess. Both were ethnic Jews, although only Hess identified openly as a Jew while Marx attempted to distance himself from his Jewish identity and embraced atheism.
>
> From the work of these two men, one may trace a multitude of communist aspects that can be tied directly to Jewish philosophies, particularly those expressed in the *Talmud*—a collection of Rabbinic writings that constitute the authoritative text on Jewish theology and philosophy. While the Talmud covers a wide array of different topics, contempt for Gentiles (non-Jews, and particularly Christians) and a belief in Jewish supremacy are pervasive themes. This spirit of Jewish supremacy is decidedly materialistic and utopian; it was precisely this attitude that characterized Marx's thinking, even while Marx rejected the Zionism of his mentor."

Marx's brand of communism—Marxism—didn't have much immediate effect, at least until it gained some new fans: Russian men, like Vladimir Lenin (in 1888) and Leon Trotsky (in 1897). As it happens, Lenin was a quarter-Jew, and Trotsky—born Lev Bronstein—was a full Jew.

In 1903, at a congress of Russian socialists, Lenin and Trotsky created a "Bolshevik" ('majority') form of communism that demanded violent revolution to overthrow existing governments. Thus was born *Bolshevism*—a particularly violent form of Marxism. And it was inspired and run by Jews.

Within just 15 years, Russian Bolshevik Jews were ready to take over the nation. In October 1917, Lenin, Trotsky, and others were able to topple the Russian government in their "Bolshevik Revolution," and thus take power. Once in charge, they installed fellow Jews at the highest levels of government—and not Russian Jews, but European and American Jews.

Here is what US ambassador David Francis wrote in January 1918:

> *"The Bolshevik leaders here [in Russia], most of whom are Jews and 90% of whom are returned exiles, care little for Russia or any other country, but are internationalists, and they are trying to start a worldwide social revolution".*[1]

About a year later, US military intelligence officer Montgomery Schuyler wrote these words to his commander:

> "It is probably unwise to say this loudly in the US, but the Bolshevik movement is, and has been since its beginning, guided and controlled by Russian Jews of the greasiest type…" (1 Mar 1919)

> "[I am worried] by the gradual gains in power of the more irresponsible and socialistic elements of the population guided by the Jews and other anti-Russian races. A table made in April 1918 by [journalist] Robert Wilton, shows that, at this time, there were 384 'commissars,' including 2 negroes, 13 Russians, 15 Chinamen, 22 Armenians, and more than 300 Jews. Of the latter number, 264 had come to Russia from the US…" (9 Jun 1919)[2]

Even Jewish journals of the time acknowledged this fact. Here are some words from *The American Hebrew* in 1920 (September 10):

> "[The Russian Revolution] was largely the outcome of Jewish thinking, of Jewish discontent, of Jewish effort to reconstruct. ... The Bolshevik movement is neither polite nor tolerant; in its initial phase, it was purely destructive. Force was needed to clear the Russian ground... What Jewish idealism and Jewish discontent have so powerfully contributed to accomplish in Russia, the same historic qualities of the Jewish mind and heart are tending to promote in other countries. ...
>
> [E]very nation [and] every civilization has the kind of Jews it deserves".[3]

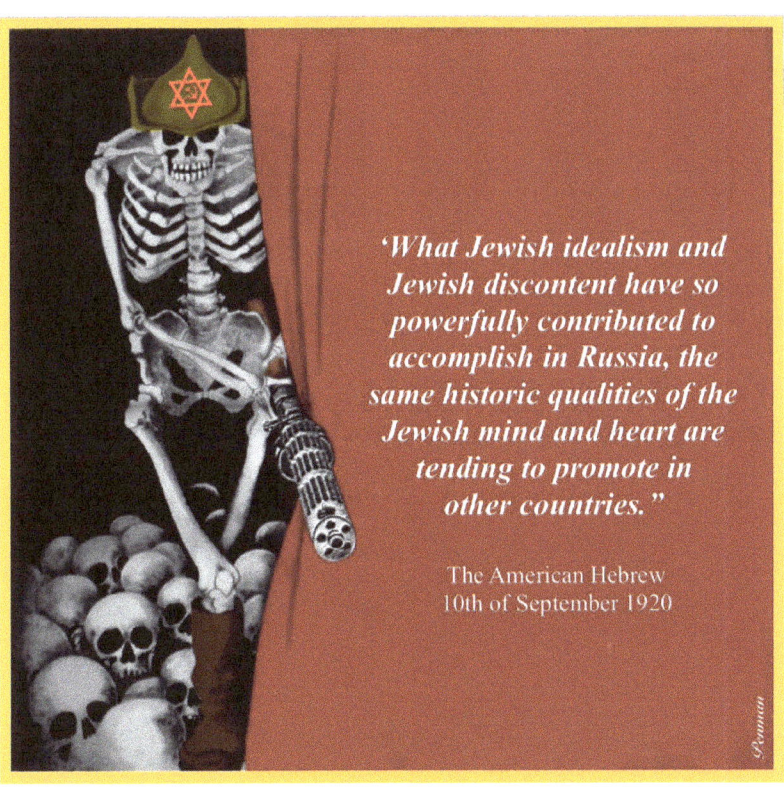

With Lenin and Trotsky in charge, Jews rapidly assumed many positions of power in the new Soviet Union. We must keep in mind that Jews made up only about 4% of the Russian Empire in the late 1800s, and yet, by 1920, they held 50%, 70%, even 90% of top jobs. The following bar graph gives some idea of the situation:[4]

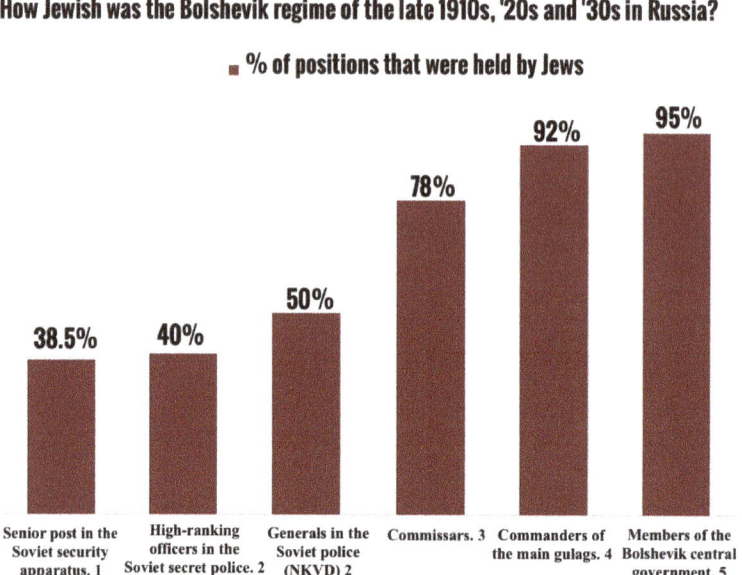

In 1924, Jewish writer Maurice Samuel admitted the Jewish tendency for destruction, something that was almost inborn in Jews:

> *"We Jews, we, the destroyers, will remain the destroyers forever. Nothing that you do will meet our needs and demands. We will forever destroy because we need a world of our own..."*[5]

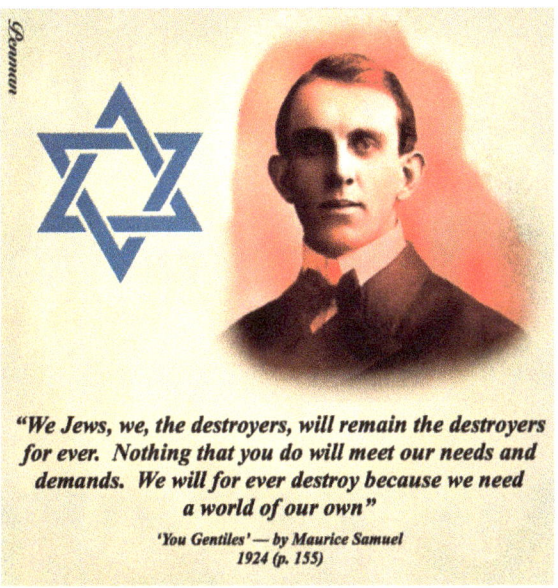

"*We Jews, we, the destroyers, will remain the destroyers for ever. Nothing that you do will meet our needs and demands. We will for ever destroy because we need a world of our own*"

'*You Gentiles*' — *by Maurice Samuel*
1924 (p. 155)

Years later, in 1961, Jewish researcher Leonard Schapiro assessed the Bolshevik situation this way:

> "[After the 1917 Revolution], times were confused, novel, bewildering, and intoxicating... Thousands of Jews thronged to the Bolsheviks, seeing in them the most determined champions of the revolution, and the most reliable internationalists. By the time the Bolsheviks seized power, Jewish participation at the highest level of the party was far from insignificant—among them, Trotsky and Yakov Sverdlov, [who was] the real master of the secretarial apparatus of the party. ... Trotsky was now second only to Lenin, and ranked high above his other colleagues in influence.
>
> [Furthermore], Jews abounded at the lower levels of the party machinery—especially in the Cheka [secret police] and its successors, the GPU, the OGPU, and the NKVD.
>
> The most prominent and colorful figure after Lenin was Trotsky, [and] in Petrograd, the dominant and hated figure was [the Jew] Grigory Zinoviev, while anyone who had the misfortune to fall into the hands of the Cheka stood a very

good chance of finding himself confronted with, and possibly shot by, a Jewish investigator".[6]

Among other crimes, the Soviet Jews, once in power, decided to ban all criticism of Jews; they made "anti-Semitism" illegal. And worse: they eventually issued *the death penalty* for it! As Benjamin Pinkus wrote, "in 1927, a decision was reached to take drastic steps to repress anti-Semitism".[7] This was confirmed by Stalin in 1931. He wrote:

> "Communists, as consistent internationalists, cannot but be irreconcilable, sworn enemies of anti-Semitism. In the USSR, anti-Semitism is punishable with the utmost severity of the law as a phenomenon deeply hostile to the Soviet system. Under USSR law, active anti-Semites are liable to the death penalty".[8]

That's one sure way to stop criticism of Jews: kill the critics!

Zionism: The Other Arm of Jewish World Domination

Also starting in the late 19th century was another Jewish movement called *Zionism*. ('Zion' is mentioned in the Old Testament—the Jewish Bible—as a hill near Jerusalem.)

Theodor Herzl (1860-1904) was a Jewish-Hungarian journalist and the father of modern political Zionism. In 1896, he published the book *Der Judenstaat* ('The Jewish State'), that argued that Jews needed to have their own nation, preferably in the Middle East. In that book, he outlined the general Jewish strategy: where Jews lacked real power, they would be radical revolutionaries; where they had power, they would use their considerable financial resources to pull strings:

> "When we sink, we become a revolutionary proletariat, the subordinate officers of the revolutionary party; when we rise, there rises also our terrible power of the purse".[9]

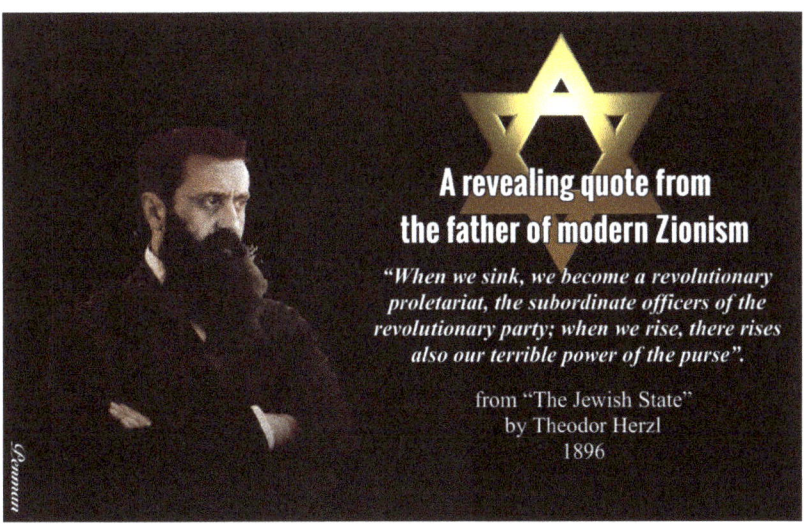

Herzl also assembled the first Zionist Congress in Basel, Switzerland, in 1897. The famous "Protocols of the Elders of Zion" are purported to be the minutes of this meeting.[10]

Herzl's "revolutionary proletariat" came to fruition with Lenin and Trotsky's Bolshevism, achieving phenomenal "success" in destroying the Russian government and conducting a brutal civil war that killed millions. This "success" was then exported to other nations, notably in Europe and in Ottoman Turkey.

By 1912, influential Jews were well-situated to press for radical revolution anywhere that they might profit from it. They had a major hand in the 1912 US presidential election, where they financially supported all three major candidates.[11] As we know, Woodrow Wilson would win that election. And via Chaim Weizmann and Herbert Samuel in Britain and Max Nordau in France, Zionist Jews had high-level influence in Europe.

When World War One broke out in 1914, the US was nominally neutral; but that didn't last for long. Wilson's Jewish backers pushed for US involvement on the side of the UK and against Germany, and eventually, in April 1917, he yielded to Jewish pressure and entered the war.

Even so, for most of that war, the Germans prevailed. The front was always far from their homeland, and their enemies—Russia to the East and England and France to the west—never made progress on the ground. Then came the Russian Bolshevik Revolution in October 1917, causing Russia to pull out of the war. This was a godsend to Germany because it allowed them to focus all military might on the Western front.

By November, the Brits were in a panic. They were in bad shape, and willing to sell their soul to the devil in order to avoid losing. Thus it happened that they yielded to the Zionist Jews and signed:

The Balfour Declaration

This "declaration"—really, just a short one-page letter—stated the British "sympathy with Jewish Zionist aspirations" and promised them "the establishment in Palestine of a national home for the Jewish people." The Brits did this as a *quid pro quo*, or a return of favors, for the Jews bringing the US into the war earlier that year. British historian Howard Temperley famously called the situation "a contract with Jewry."

This declaration was very cleverly worded; it did not give the Arabs political rights, it did not stipulate what the boundaries of Palestine were, and it used the word 'homeland' which had not existed in international law until then.

The other part of the "contract" involved German Jews becoming, once again, radical revolutionaries in order to attack Germany from within. The first blow came in July 1918, when a Russian Jew assassinated the German ambassador Von Mirbach in Moscow. Then in October came labor strikes in German shipyards and munitions factories. A general strike then spread to Munich, and by early November, Kaiser Wilhelm was compelled to abdicate. The Jewish rebels then formed a new "German Republic" and promptly surrendered, thus ending World War One.

This is how the Jews committed the infamous "stab in the back" that cost Germany the war.

Incidentally, we still have many Zionists around the world today, decades after WW2. These modern-day Zionists are mostly concerned with protecting and enriching the state of Israel, which was created in 1948. They direct billions in "foreign aid" to Israel, they push for military action against Israel's enemies, and they provide political cover by censoring or ignoring Israeli crimes against humanity in Palestine and elsewhere around the world.

Hitler Comes to Power

Among the thousands of active German soldiers in World War One who deeply felt the "stab in the back" was a young, 29-year-old frontline infantryman named Adolf Hitler. He had fought for nearly four years in the war, and suffered at least two major injuries on the battlefield. At the time of the German "surrender," he was in the small town of Pasewalk recovering from a gas attack on his division in Belgium.

Upon hearing the news of the surrender, Hitler was crushed. He wrote about this tragic event in his great work, *Mein Kampf*. I quote him here in a lengthy passage from Chapter 7:

> With the next few days came the most terrible information of my life. The rumors grew more and more persistent. What I had taken as a local affair was, in reality, a general revolution. In addition to this, shameful news came from the front. They wanted to capitulate. Was such a thing possible?
>
> On November 10 the local pastor gave a short address at the hospital; now we learned the whole story.
>
> I was in a state of extreme agitation as I listened to the address. The reverend old gentleman seemed to be trembling as he informed us that the House of Hohenzollern would no longer wear the imperial crown. The Fatherland had become a 'Republic,' and we should pray to the Almighty to grant us his blessing in the new order of things and to not abandon our people in the days to come. In delivering his speech, he couldn't do more than briefly express appreciation to the royal house, its services to Pomerania, to Prussia, indeed, to the whole of the German Fatherland, and—here he began to weep. A feeling of profound dismay fell upon the people in that little hall, and I don't think there was a single dry eye in the crowd.
>
> As for myself, I broke down completely when the old gentleman tried to resume his story by informing us that we must now end this long war. The war was lost, he said, and

we were at the mercy of the victor. The Fatherland would have to bear heavy burdens in the future. We were to accept the terms of the armistice, and trust in the magnanimity of our former enemies. It was impossible for me to stay and listen any longer. Darkness surrounded me as I staggered and stumbled back to my ward and buried my aching head into the blankets and pillow.

I hadn't cried since the day I stood beside my mother's grave. Whenever fate dealt cruelly with me in my youth, my spirit of determination grew stronger. During all those long years of war, when death claimed many friends and comrades, it would have been almost sinful to have uttered a word of complaint—they died for Germany! And finally, in the last few days of that titanic struggle, when the waves of poison gas enveloped me and began to penetrate my eyes, and the thought of becoming permanently blind unnerved me, my voice of conscience cried out: 'Miserable fellow, will you start howling when there are thousands of others whose lot is a hundred times worse than yours?' And so I accepted my misfortune in silence, realizing that nothing else could be done, and that my personal suffering was nothing compared with the misfortune of the Fatherland.

The horrible reality landed upon him: all his fighting, all the sacrifices made at the front, all the lives lost—all was in vain, thanks to the Jewish criminals in the homeland. He continued:

> In vain all the sacrifices and privations; in vain the hunger and thirst for endless months; in vain those hours that we stuck to our posts even though mortal fear gripped our souls; and in vain the deaths of two million. Of those hundreds of thousands who set out with hearts full of faith in their Fatherland, and never returned—shouldn't their graves now open, so that the spirits of those heroes splattered with mud and blood may come home and take vengeance on those who had so despicably betrayed the greatest sacrifice that a human being can make for his country? Was it for this that the soldiers died in August and September 1914? For this, that the volunteer regiments followed the old comrades in the autumn of the same year? For this, that those boys of 17 sank into the earth of Flanders? Was this the meaning of the sacrifice that German mothers made for their Fatherland when, with heavy hearts, they said goodbye to their sons who never returned? Has all this been done so that a gang of despicable criminals could lay their hands on the Fatherland? […]
>
> Despicable and degenerate criminals!
>
> The more I tried to gain some clarity on this monstrous event, the more my head burned with rage and shame. What was the pain in my eyes compared with this tragedy?
>
> The following days were terrible to bear, and the nights worse still. I knew that all was lost. Only fools, liars, or criminals could depend on the mercy of the enemy. During those nights, my hatred grew—hatred for the originators of this crime.

The tragedy of that time profoundly changed the young man. He now realized the true danger of the Marxist Jews who had been allowed to run rampant in Germany. As a result, his life's mission became clear:

> In the days that followed, my own fate became clear to me. I had to laugh at the thought of my personal future, which only recently was the cause of so much concern. Was it not ridiculous to build something on such a foundation? Finally, it became clear that the inevitable had happened, something that I had long feared, though I didn't have the heart to believe it.
>
> Kaiser Wilhelm II was the first German Emperor to offer the hand of friendship to the Marxist leaders, not suspecting that they were scoundrels without honor. While they held the imperial hand in theirs, the other hand was already reaching for the dagger.
>
> There is no coming to agreement with the Jews, but rather only the hard 'either-or'.[12]

It was this event that caused Hitler to enter politics, in order to avenge the traitorous stab-in-the-back.

Adolf Hitler

By 1920, he had formed a new political party: the National Socialist German Workers' Party (NSDAP). Their enemies called them "Nazis."

All the while, the heavily-Jewish "Weimar government" ruled Germany—with tragic results. In the 1920s and early 1930s, Germany was drowning in debt. Inflation destroyed life savings. Countless homes and farms were lost to speculators and to private (Jewish-controlled) banks. Many Germans lived in hovels and were starving. Meanwhile, rich Jews were living it up in the "Roaring Twenties," wallowing in moral debasement and a degraded 'culture.'

The fundamentally Jewish, destructive nature of this time was captured well in 1928 by a Jewish writer, Marcus Ravage:

> You have not begun to appreciate the real depth of our guilt. We are intruders. We are disturbers. We are subverters. We have taken your natural world, your ideals, your destiny, and played havoc with them. We have been at the bottom of not merely the latest Great War but of nearly all your wars, not only of the Russian but of nearly every other major revolution in your history. We have brought discord and confusion and frustration into your personal and public life. We are still doing it.[13]

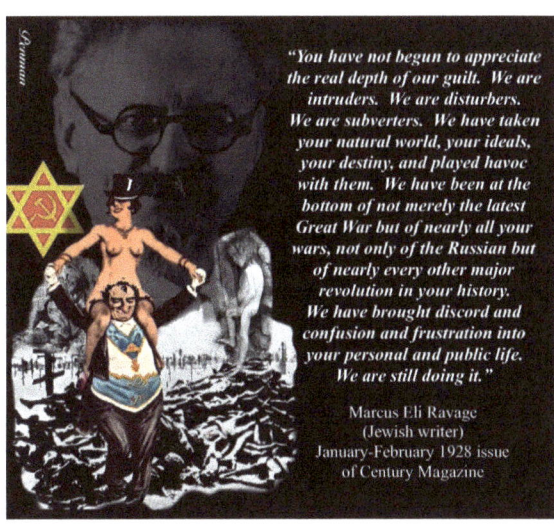

But the economic and cultural crisis had to be overcome. Hitler and his NSDAP men devised a new form of currency—a state-issued, value-based currency—that was immune to inflation and thus was a direct threat to the wealth and power of the private central banks. Armed with such economic ideas, and determined to rid Germany of the Jewish menace, Hitler's party rapidly rose to power. He loved the German people, and they loved him.

Finally, in 1933, Hitler and the NSDAP succeeded in attaining leadership of the German nation. Immediately, the international finance-Jews began organizing a global boycott against Germany to strangle this upstart ruler who thought he could break free of private central bankers. In one famous headline of that year, the Jews "of all the world" *declared war* on Germany! They would do anything to stop this man Hitler.

The lead story said:

> "Fourteen million Jews stand together as one man, to declare war against Germany. The Jewish wholesaler will forsake his firm, the banker his stock exchange, the merchant his commerce and the pauper his pitiful shed in order to join together in a holy war against Hitler's people".[14]

A "holy war" indeed! Such was the thinking of the Zionist Jews.

Yet within a few short years of coming to power, Hitler and his National Socialist government had completely transformed the country; they went from a nation in crippling debt and almost 7 million unemployed, to full employment and the highest standard of living in the world.

In just six short years—from 1933 to 1939—Hitler's Germany rose from the depths of despair, and, amidst a global Depression that was crippling other industrial nations, became a true world power. In just six short years, Germany went from a Jewish-run plutocracy to the strongest nation on Earth.

The Second World War

Confronted with Hitler's spectacular success in Germany, no doubt due in large part to his derailing of Jewish power there, Jews around the world became hell-bent on destroying him. Marxist, Bolshevist Jews in the USSR hated the Germans and all Europeans, and were determined spread their "global revolution" to Europe. Western, capitalist Jews hated Hitler's destruction of their banking monopolies and his rounding-up and deporting of German Jews. And of course, German Jews themselves hated Hitler because he pushed them out of power. Thus, "left, right, and center," Hitler had Jews allied against him.

As I mentioned above, Jews "declared a holy war" on Hitler already in 1933. Throughout the 1930s, American and British Jews pushed their respective leaders to become ever-more belligerent toward Germany. This, despite the fact that it was not in the interest of either England or America to fight Germany. They were never threatened by Hitler; his interest was always "to the East," where he wanted to stifle the Bolshevik threat and gain living space for the German people.

Hitler's only "war" was his invasion of Poland in order to reclaim land seized in WWI. That was a border war, not a world war. It was only when *England and France declared war on Hitler* that the war expanded. And they did so at the behest of their respective Jewish lobbies.

Who really started The Second World War?

Jewish threats made to Germany throughout the 1930's

"Hitler will have no war, but he will be forced into it"
Emil Ludwig Cohn in Les Annales, June, 1934,
also quoted in his book 'The New Holy Alliance'

The Jews Declared WAR on Germany in 1933!

"Germany is the enemy of Judaism and must be pursued with deadly hatred. The goal of Judaism of today is: a merciless campaign against all German peoples and the complete destruction of the nation. We demand a complete blockade of trade, the importation of raw materials stopped, and retaliation towards every German, woman and child."
Jewish professor A. Kulischer (October, 1937)

Germany is our public enemy number one. It is our object to declare war without mercy against her. One may be sure of this: We will lead that war!
Bernard Lecache,
the president of the 'International League Against Racism and Anti-Semitism,'
in its newspaper 'Droit de Vivre' (Right to Life), 9 November, 1938

Source: See endnotes.[15]

Prior to the wider war, Hitler had nothing but good will toward Britain. Here is an enlightening passage from *Hitler's Revolution* (2013) by Richard Tedor:

> "Once chancellor, Hitler hoped to nurture good relations with England. In January 1934, he ordered the army to return the kettle drums of the Gordon Highlanders, which the Germans had captured on the battlefield in 1914. At a ceremony in the Berlin War Ministry, the Germans presented the former trophies to Sir Jan Hamilton to restore them to their regiment in Scotland.
>
> Hitler also concluded the Anglo-German Naval Agreement in June 1935, which imposed restrictions on German rearmament but not on England's.
>
> Hitler additionally gave a conciliatory interview to Ward Price, the European correspondent of the *Daily Mail:*
>
> *"On 4 August 1914, I was very distressed that the two great Germanic peoples, who had lived at peace with one another throughout all the disputes and fluctuations in human history for so many centuries, were drawn into war. I would be pleased if this unfortunate atmosphere would finally come to an end and the two related nations could rediscover their old friendship. The assertion that the German people are enthusiastically preparing for war is a misunderstanding of the German revolution. We find it simply incomprehensible. We leaders of the German nation had almost without exception been front-line soldiers. I would like to see the front-line soldier who wants to prepare for another war."*

But the Brits never returned his feelings of good will. As early as 1936, Churchill was quoted as saying "Germany is getting too strong. We must smash her".[16] Then in 1938, a full year before the war, Churchill said this to Roosevelt's Jewish advisor Bernard Baruch:

> "War is coming very soon. We will be in it and you will be in it. You [Baruch] will be running the show over there, but I will be on the sidelines over here".[17]

So, the American Jews would be "running the show," and the Brits would simply be "on the sidelines," waiting for orders.

Then in December of 1938, British Lord Beaverbrook made this claim:

> "The Jews are after [Prime Minister] Chamberlain. He is being terribly harassed by them… All the Jews are against him… They have got a big position in the press here [in the UK]… I am shaken. The Jews may drive us into war [and] their political influence is moving us in that direction".[18]

What about on the American side? Consider this report by Jerzy Potocki, the Polish ambassador to the US, who wrote back to Warsaw in early 1938:

> "The pressure of the Jews on President Roosevelt and on the State Department is becoming ever more powerful... The Jews are right now the leaders in creating a war psychosis which would plunge the entire world into war and bring about general catastrophe. This mood is becoming more and more apparent. In their definition of democratic states, the Jews have also created real chaos; they have mixed together the idea of democracy and communism, and have above all raised the banner of burning hatred against Nazism".[19]

This was confirmed in a letter by US senator Hiram Johnson:

> "All the Jews [are] on one side, wildly enthusiastic for the President, and willing to fight to the last American".[20]

Triumph of the Truth 31

Documents clearly establish Roosevelt's crucial role in planning and instigating World War II

"There is a feeling now prevalent in the United States marked by growing hatred of Fascism, and above all of Chancellor Hitler and everything connected with National Socialism. Propaganda is mostly in the hands of the Jews, who control almost 100% of radio, film, daily and periodical press."

**From a secret report dated 12 January 1939,
by Jerzy Potocki,
the Polish ambassador to the United States.**

By early 1939, the situation was becoming dire. Potocki again reported back to his superiors in Poland:

> "The feeling now prevailing in the United States is marked by a growing hatred of Fascism and, above all, of Chancellor Hitler and everything connected with Nazism. Propa-

ganda is mostly in the hands of the Jews, who control almost 100 percent of radio, film, daily and periodical press.

It is interesting to note that in this extremely well-planned campaign which is conducted above all against National Socialism, Soviet Russia is almost completely excluded. If mentioned at all, it is only in a friendly manner and things are presented in such a way as if Soviet Russia were working with the bloc of democratic states. Thanks to the clever propaganda the sympathy of the American public is completely on the side of Red Spain. Besides this propaganda, a war psychosis is being artificially created".[21]

Next, let's look at the thoughts of Joseph Kennedy—US ambassador to the UK and father of JFK. In mid-1939, Kennedy was quoted in a British journal as "privately telling his English friends in the Cliveden set that the Jews were running the United States." It also stated that Kennedy believed that "the democratic policy of the United States is a Jewish production".[22]

Finally, consider this letter from leading British Jew, Chaim Weizmann, sent directly to PM Chamberlain on 29 August 1939—four days *before* the start of the war:

"I wish to confirm in the most explicit manner the declarations which I and my colleagues have made during the last month and especially in the last week: *that the Jews stand by Great Britain and will fight on the side of the democracies.*

Our urgent desire is to give effect to these declarations. We wish to do so in a way entirely consonant with the general scheme of British action and, therefore, would place ourselves, in matters big and small, under the coordinating direction of His Majesty's Government. The Jewish Agency is ready to enter into *immediate arrangements* for utilizing *Jewish manpower, technical ability and resources*, etc."[23]

I think we don't really need to ask: Who started this war?

What About "the Holocaust"?

Ok, sure, maybe the Jews pushed for war, both in the US and the UK. And maybe they hated Hitler. But still, that doesn't excuse the Holocaust, does it? That doesn't excuse killing 6 million Jews, does it?

But what if 6 million Jews *weren't* killed? What if that famous number was *just a symbol*, representing "lots of Jews"? What if that number had been in circulation for years before WW2, *and even before WW1*, to describe "lots of suffering Jews"?

The New York Times
Expect the World®

"Holocaust" and "6 million Jews" stories brought to you ever since 1869 by Jew-owned "Newspaper of Record"

When you look at documented history and see decades of "6 million suffering Jews," you realize that the Jews are flamboyant liars, and don't care at all for factual truth.

But what about those gas chambers? We all know the story: that the "Nazis" killed millions of Jews in gas chambers at Auschwitz. Actually, that is not true at all. In fact, it was technically impossible to kill millions of Jews that way.

Here is what the American gas chamber expert, Fred Leuchter, said:

> Construction of these facilities further shows that they were never used as gas chambers. None of these facilities were sealed or gasketed. No provision was ever made to prevent condensation of gas on the walls, floor, or ceiling. No provision ever existed to exhaust the air-gas mixture from these buildings. No provision ever existed to introduce or distribute the gas throughout the chamber. No explosion-proof lighting existed and no attempt was ever made to prevent gas from entering the crematories, even though the gas is highly explosive. No attempt was made to protect operating personnel from exposure to the gas or to protect other non-participating persons from exposure.
>
> Specifically, at Auschwitz, a floor drain in the alleged gas chamber was connected directly to the camp's storm drain system. At Majdanek, a depressed walkway around the alleged gas chambers would have collected gas seepage and resulted in a death trap for camp personnel. No exhaust stacks ever existed.
>
> Hydrogen cyanide ("Zyklon") gas is an extremely dangerous and lethal gas, and nowhere were there any provisions to effect any amount of safe handling. The chambers were too small to accommodate more than a small fraction of the alleged numbers. *Plain and simple, these facilities could not have operated as execution gas chambers.*[24]

But lots of people died, right? We have photos of piles of corpses—are they fakes? How did those people die?

Sure, many people died in the German camps—hundreds or thousands, depending on the camp. But in virtually all cases, we don't know (a) Who those people were, or (b) How they died. Were they Jews, or Soviets, or other prisoners? Were they shot? Did they die of disease like typhus?

Here is an assessment by one recent writer:

> "The horrific scenes encountered by U.S. and British troops when they entered German concentration camps at the end of World War II have been used to prove a German policy of extermination of the Jews.

As gruesome as these scenes were, it was soon discovered that most of the deaths in the German camps were caused by disease and other natural causes. None of the autopsy reports show that anyone died of poison gas. Also, contrary to publicized claims, no researcher has been able to document a German policy of extermination through starvation in the German camps. The virtual collapse of Germany's food, transport, and public health systems and the extreme overcrowding in the German camps at the end of the war led to the catastrophe the Allied troops encountered when they entered the camps".[25]

Another recent and more specialized commentator, Samuel Crowell, confirms this conclusion:

"No autopsy from any camp has ever yielded a verdict of cyanide poisoning. ... The most troubling aspect of the mass gassing claim is not that it was made on the basis of slender or non-existent evidence. It is rather that *nothing* has been produced over the past 50 years that supports the claim.

In the past several years, numerous archives have been opened to study, and the British government has released many of its ULTRA decrypts for scholarly use along with the transcripts of conversations among detained Germans that were secretly recorded. The tapes and decrypts indicate a knowledge of mass shootings as far back as the summer of 1941, as well as the confessions of SS officers who took part in such procedures, as well as secret concentration camp radio traffic, including that of Auschwitz, but there is *nothing* in any of these materials about gassing".[26]

Based on the little physical evidence that we do have, and based on essential facts of chemistry and physics, and based on existing documentary and photographic evidence, it appears that most estimates of Jewish deaths are about 10x too high. The actual Jewish death toll in the "Holocaust" appears to be about 500,000—far below the claimed 6M.[27]

War's End, and Post-War

Under assault from all sides, and faced with the combined military of several major enemy nations, the German forces began to retreat in late 1943. They steadily lost ground in 1944, and by early 1945 they were near collapse. The Allies, meanwhile—especially the US and the Brits—conducted increasingly brutal air attacks against civilian targets. They fire-bombed innocent cities, simply as "punishment," and thus killed thousands of women, children, and elderly.

Here are just a few of the Allied targets, and the estimated death toll:

- Hamburg (July 1943)—around 45,000 civilians killed.
- Kassel (October 1943)—around 10,000 killed.
- Darmstadt (September 1944)—around 12,000 killed.
- Dresden (February 1945)—up to 50,000 killed.
- Pforzheim (February 1945)—around 17,000 killed.

Even as the poor Dresdners had to pile up and burn their dead women and children, British and American media worked hard to cover up news of such war crimes.

As proof, I recall here one letter to the BBC and the higher clergy from the British Ministry of Information:

> *Sir, I am directed by the Ministry to send you the following circular letter:*
>
> *It is often the duty of the good citizens and of the pious Christians to turn a blind eye on the peculiarities of those associated with us. But the time comes when such peculiarities, while still denied in public, must be taken into account when action by us is called for. ...*
>
> *We must, therefore, take into account how the Red Army will certainly behave when it overruns Central Europe. Unless precautions are taken, the obviously inevitable horrors which will result will throw an undue strain on public opinion in this country. We cannot reform the Bolsheviks but we can do our best to save them—and ourselves—from the consequences of their acts. The disclosures of the past quarter of a century will render mere denials unconvincing. The only alternative to denial is to distract public attention from the whole subject. Experience has shown that the best distraction is atrocity propaganda directed against the enemy.*
>
> *Unfortunately, the public is no longer so susceptible as in the days of the "Corpse Factory," and the "Mutilated Belgian Babies," and the "Crucified Canadians."*
>
> *Your cooperation is therefore earnestly sought to distract public attention from the doings of the Red Army by your wholehearted support of various charges against the Germans and Japanese which have been and will be put into circulation by the Ministry. Your expression of belief in such may convince others. I am, Sir, Your obedient servant,*
> (signed) H. HEWET, ASSISTANT SECRETARY[28]

In other words:
- We all know about the crimes committed by the Bolsheviks over the last 24 years in Russia and Eastern Europe.
- It is inevitable they will do the same in Central Europe.

- We will cover up their crimes by lying about the Germans.
- The public is not as stupid as it once was, therefore our lies need to be better.
- You (the BBC and the Anglican Church) must help spread these lies, and do so convincingly.

In all, up to 200,000 German civilians were killed in what can only be called Allied war crimes. Not only that, but the invading Soviets were notorious rapists of the helpless female population. Here is one recent story on the BBC website:

> "Based on contemporary hospital reports and on surging abortion rates in the following months, it is estimated that up to two million German women were raped during the last six months of World War Two, around 100,000 of them in Berlin".[29]

Yet more war crimes by the noble "victors."

And all along, Jews in the Allied nations were calling for more destruction, more death. One of the worst was the Soviet Jew Ilya Ehrenburg; he was a truly pathological and demented person, someone for whom no amount of killing of civilians was sufficient.

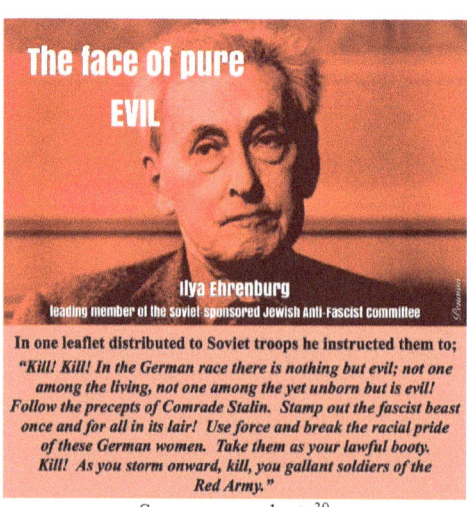

Source: see endnote[30]

Also rampant during the war were Jewish media lies, constructed mostly in the UK, by such devious men as Denis Sefton Delmer. This Australian Jew was raised in Berlin and thus was fluent in German. He became Britain's chief of "black propaganda" during the war. In his postwar book, Delmer recalled telling his team:

> "We must never lie by accident, or through slovenliness, only deliberately! … [W]e are up to all the dirty tricks we can devise. No holds are barred. The dirtier, the better. Lies, treachery, everything".[31]

HOW THE ALLIES SPREAD LIES TO RUIN GERMANY

"We shall continue this atrocity propaganda, we shall intensify it, until nobody shall accept a good word from the Germans anymore, until all the sympathy you had in other countries shall be destroyed..."

— *D. Sefton Delmer*

Just after the war, Delmer met with a German lawyer, Friedrich Grimm. Grimm said:

> "[In WWI, there were] magazines showing artificial corpse mountains by photomontage composed of dummies. These pictures were distributed, with a space left for caption. It was given out by telephone later on according to the needs from the propaganda centre.
>
> Thereby I pulled out one of the [WW2] leaflets exhibiting allegedly mountains of dead bodies out of the concentration camps, and showed it to my visitor [Delmer], who looked at me, taken aback.

> I cannot imagine that in this war with all weapons perfected to such an extent, this mentally toxic weapon should have been neglected that decided the outcome of World War I. More so, I know it for sure! …
>
> First were reported hundreds of corpses in the concentration camps, then six weeks later when it was the turn of this same country again, thousands, then ten thousand, then a hundred thousand. Here I thought to myself: This number inflation cannot possibly skyrocket to a million!
>
> Now I reached for another leaflet: "Here you have a million!" There my visitor [Delmer] blurted out: "I see, I have run into an expert. Now I also want to tell you, who I am. I am not a university professor. I am of the central office you talked about: Atrocity propaganda—and with it we won total victory."
>
> I replied: "I know, and now you must stop it!" Delmer retorted: "No, now we shall start all the more! We shall continue this atrocity propaganda, we shall intensify it, until nobody shall accept a good word from the Germans anymore, until all the sympathy you had in other countries shall be destroyed, and until the Germans themselves shall be so confused that they do not know anymore what they are doing!"[32]

Not only the Germans, but a few highly-placed Americans could also see through the fraud and propaganda. One of these was US general George Patton.

In the immediate aftermath of the war, Patton was brought in to help address the problem of 'displaced persons' (DP), of whom there were many thousands—and many Jews. It was this, combined with his first-hand experience of what the Allies had done to Germany, that caused him to dramatically change his views.

PATTON DISCOVERED THE TRUTH ABOUT THE WAR WITH GERMANY

"...the Jews, who are lower than animals."

"[T]hese Jewish DPs...have no sense of human relationships."

"I have never looked at a group of people who seem to be more lacking in intelligence and spirit."

Patton's honest thoughts on Germany and the Jews are recorded in his published diary. There, we find these entries:

- "[General] Harrison and his ilk believe that the Displaced Person is a human being, which he is not, and this applies particularly to the Jews, who are lower than animals. I remember once at Troina in Sicily, General Gay said that it wasn't a question of the people living with the dirty animals but of the animals living with the dirty people. At that time, he had never seen a Displaced Jew." (15 Sep 1945)

Things got worse for Patton a couple days later:

- "[T]hese Jewish DPs, or at least a majority of them, have no sense of human relationships. They decline, where practicable, to use latrines, preferring to relieve themselves on the floor. ...
    This happened to be the feast of Yom Kippur, so they were all collected in a large wooden building which they called a synagogue. We entered the synagogue, which was packed with the greatest stinking bunch of humanity I have ever seen. ... [T]he smell was so terrible that I almost fainted and actually about

- three hours later lost my lunch as a result of remembering it." (17 Sep 1945)
- "It is an unfortunate fact that the people at home [in the US] who are so vociferous in their demands for the betterment of the Displaced Jews have no conception of the low mental, moral, and physical standards of the objects of their solicitude…" (30 Sep)

The "vociferousness" of the Americans was due, in large part, to a Jewish presence in the media: "There is a very apparent Semitic influence in the press," he said.

Oddly, Patton would not live much longer. He was involved in a minor car accident on December 9, hospitalized, and then suddenly died on December 21, of "congestive heart failure," at age 60.

*****

But wait…we had those Nuremberg Trials after the war. Didn't that prove all the "Nazi" war crimes? Didn't that prove the "Holocaust"? The Germans even admitted it! We have it all in writing!

Again, wrong. In all the Nuremberg documentation, we have no evidence of a Holocaust, no evidence of gas chambers, no evidence of "6 million Jews." True, we have *claims* of these things; *but claims are not evidence*. Anyone can make a claim about anything. And many Germans did—under extreme duress.

Let's look at what one American judge, Edward van Roden, said after he investigated the situation in Germany.

Van Roden was assigned to investigate claims of abuse by American prosecutors at Dachau, who had allegedly tortured German prisoners to obtain confessions and incriminating statements. The lead American was a Jew, William Perl.

According to Van Roden, Perl said, "We had a tough case to crack and we had to use persuasive methods." These methods included such "expedients" as "some violence" and "mock trials." The infographic below contains more of what Van Roden said.

Judge Condemns methods of obtaining confessions at Nuremberg trials

Pennsylvania judge Edward L. Van Roden

"The statements which were admitted as evidence were obtained from men who had first been kept in solitary confinement for three, four, and five months. They were confined between four walls, with no windows, and no opportunity of exercise. Two meals a day were shoved into them through a slot in the door. They were not allowed to talk to anyone. They had no communication with their families or any minister or priest during that time.

This solitary confinement proved sufficient in itself in some cases to persuade the Germans to sign prepared statements. These statements not only involved the signer, but often would involve other defendants.

Our investigators would put a black hood over the accused's head and then punch him in the face with rubber hose. Many of the German defendants had teeth knocked out. Some had their jaws broken.

All but two of the Germans, in the 139 cases we investigated, had been kicked in the testicles beyond repair. This was Standard Operating Procedure with American investigators.

These statements were confirmed by writer Freda Utley in her 1949 book, *The High Cost of Vengeance*. She wrote:

> "[It seemed] strange and horrible that we should sit in judgement on the Germans who never succeeded in killing nearly so many civilians as we did, or in perpetrating worse atrocities than our obliteration bombing of whole cities, [such as] Dresden, where we inflicted the most horrible death imaginable on a quarter of a million people in one night…
>
> [T]here was no crime the Nazis had committed, which we or our allies had not also committed."

She recounts the various details of Van Roden's investigation and the subsequent findings of massive abuse and torture. She then adds:

> "How many of the men America has hung, and is hanging now week by week, were innocent, will never be known. Only one thing is certain: they never had a fair trial, and their interrogation, condemnation, and execution are a disgrace to democratic justice."

Similar stories were told about nearly all the Nuremberg trials. How many "confessions" and "statements" were the result of torture, we will never know.

Criticize the Jews? Never!

Recall that I mentioned that, back in the late 1920s, the Soviets applied the death penalty to anyone guilty of "anti-Semitism." Dr. Joseph Goebbels noted this fact in his diary, on a number of occasions. For example, on 19 Apr 1943, he wrote:

> "The Jews in England are now calling for legal protection against anti-Semitism. We know that from our own past, in the times of struggle. But even that didn't give them much advantage. We've always understood how to find gaps in these protective laws; and moreover, anti-Semitism, once it rises from the depths of the people, cannot be broken by law. *A law against Jew-hatred is usually the beginning of the end for the Jews.*"

In a late essay, "Creators of the World's Misfortunes," Dr. Goebbels wrote the following:

> "Capitalism and Bolshevism have the same Jewish roots—two branches of the same tree that in the end bear the same fruit. International Jewry uses both in its own way to suppress nations and keep them in its service. How deep its influence on public opinion is in all the enemy countries and many neutral nations is plain to see: it may never be mentioned in newspapers, speeches, and radio broadcasts.
>
> There's a law in the Soviet Union that punishes 'anti-Semitism'—or in plain English, public education about the Jewish Question—by death. Any expert in these matters is in no way surprised that a leading spokesman for the Kremlin said over the New Year that the Soviet Union would not rest until this law was valid throughout the world.
>
> In other words, the enemy clearly says that its goal in this war is *to put the total domination of Jewry over the nations of the Earth under legal protection*, and to use the death penalty to threaten even a discussion of this shameful attempt. It is little different in the plutocratic [Western] nations."

And in one of his very last diary entries, he wrote:

> "The Jews have already registered for the San Francisco Conference [on post-war plans]. It is characteristic that their main demand is to ban anti-Semitism throughout the world. Typically, having committed the most terrible crimes against mankind, the Jews would now like mankind to be forbidden even to think about them".[33]

Little has changed, even 80 years later. There is no death penalty, but there is 'virtual death': cancel culture, firings from jobs, lawsuits, physical attacks, slander, you name it.

ASK YOURSELF THIS ...

Suppose after Napoleon's final defeat at the battle of Waterloo in 1815, the allied powers who had finally defeated Napoleon decided to create laws that made it illegal to question any part of the official narrative of the wars that were fought against The French Empire between the years 1805 to 1815.

To put forward any view that went against the official story, even if backed by vast amounts of research and evidence, would have you in prison, and ruined. How outrageous would that be?

> *But let us further suppose those laws were still in place today! It would be far beyond outrageous; it would be a crime against humanity that we could never talk freely about such events.*
>
> *Yet, after the Second World War, one group of people, with enormous influence and financial power, has made it illegal to question their story of the Second World War. In many nations, there are prison sentences, regardless of how much documented evidence is brought forward by anyone who questions the official narrative! Even in countries without such laws, one's livelihood could be ruined by expressing any doubts regarding the Jewish version of the Second World War!*
>
> *Is this not outrageous? Will such insane laws still be in effect a decade from now? A century? Forever?*

This is the situation with the Holocaust, with Hitler, and with National Socialism. No dissent is allowed. If you are a prominent person and you say the wrong thing, you will grovel for forgiveness or you will be ruined. Wealthy Jews, influential Jews, the ADL, Gentile lackeys who work for Jews—they will attack you, often unseen, and try to destroy your life. And they *must* do this, because the truth is not on their side. Censorship, slander, attacks, and imprisonment are their only tools.

For the global Jewish Lobby, the truth is dangerous. And worse: it could mean the end of their power and the end of their dominance.

There are even a few brave Jewish writers who acknowledge this. One is Gerard Menuhin, in his book *Tell the Truth and Shame the Devil* (2015):

Laws to prevent questions

Alone the fact that one may not question the Jewish "holocaust" and that Jewish pressure has inflicted laws on democratic societies to prevent questions—while incessant promotion and indoctrination of the same averredly incontestable 'holocaust' occur—gives the game away. It proves that it must be a lie. Why else would one not be allowed to question it? Because it might offend the "survivors"? Because it "dishonors the dead"? Hardly sufficient reason to outlaw discussion. No, because the exposure of this leading lie might precipitate questions about so many other lies and cause the whole ramshackle fabrication to crumble.

from Tell The Truth and Shame The Devil (Published October 2015) by Gerard Menuhin (Jewish)

Tell the truth, and the lie will crumble. Destroy the Holocaust lie, and many other Jewish lies will crumble in its wake.

Looking Ahead

Such is the ugly truth. We have been lied to, deceived, and misled by a hugely false narrative about Hitler, WW2, and the Jews. Hitler never wanted a global war; he only wanted the best for his German people. He fought a titanic battle against malevolent and hate-filled Jews, to his east and to his west, in an attempt to permanently defeat this enemy of humanity. He risked all, and sacrificed all.

Yes, he lost that battle, but the larger war continues. Hitler's legacy continues. The truth will come out—it always does.

As it stands, the haters rule. For the globalist Jews—those "planetary master criminals," according to Heidegger—no war, no economic manipulation, no media distortion is too much or too extreme. For ordinary people, this is hard to understand. Ordinary people are not haters, so they have a very hard time relating to this ancient, in-born, Jewish hatred of non-Jews. It goes back centuries, even millennia.[34] And it never ends.

OPEN YOUR EYES TO THE REALITY OF WHAT IS GOING ON

Please read the below very carefully and think well upon it! The Jews will use any means—even the hated Muslims—to destroy the hated Europeans.

In a sermon uploaded directly to his Liveleak account on 20 November 2013, Rabbi David Touitou, a French-speaking Haredi rabbi, stated the following:

> *"You will pay dearly for it* [the flood of Muslim immigrants] *Europeans! To such an extent that you have no idea! And you will have no place to run to. Because all the evil you have done to Israel* [the Jews], *you will pay for it a hundred-fold. ...*

> *According to the Rafet Israim, the Gog and Magog war is that Islam in Europe will rise as one man and they have everything to succeed. This war in the world we live in is necessary. Why is it necessary? Because one is going to use the other, so that Israel does not enter war...*
>
> *What you are undergoing in France, in Europe, which is so scary, it should be for us the most beautiful news of our Jewish history. Finally, we begin to approach it! Finally, we begin to realize what the sages had predicted before. What I told you before is written in Sanhedrin* [book of the

Talmud]. *The Messiah will come only when Edom, Europe, Christianity will have fallen completely. So, I am asking you the question: Is it good news that Islam is invading Europe? It's excellent news! It's announcing the arrival of the Messiah! Excellent news!"*

This is such a sick and perverted outlook that it is difficult to know what to say. And such people run governments, run the economy, run the media.

*****

This is my story. Obviously, there is much more to be said. This is only a start, a beginning.

In closing: We would do well to recall the final words that Hitler ever wrote. In his last will and testament, written the day before he died, in the final sentence, Hitler said:

> *"Above all, I enjoin the government and the people to uphold the race laws to the limit, and to unmercilessly resist the world-poisoner of all nations, international Jewry."*

Now, today, 80 years later, it is up to us.

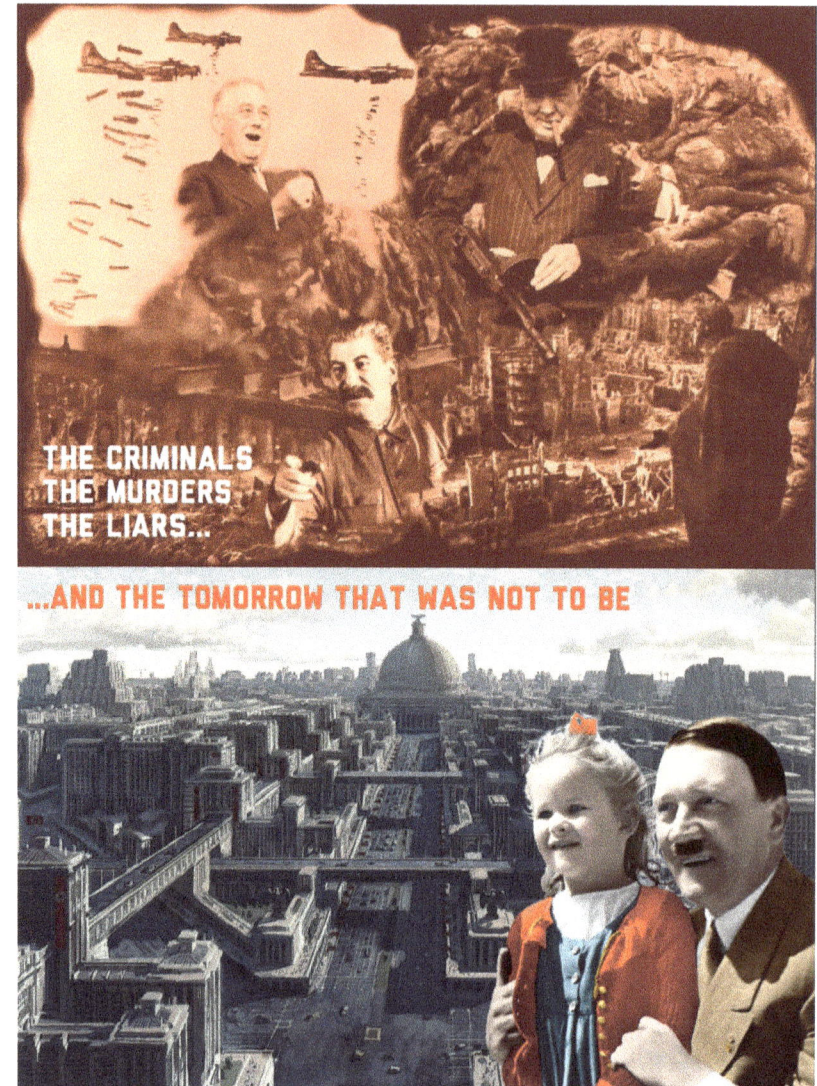

Recommended Books and Videos

There is a lot of bad information out there on these topics, much of it intentionally so. It can take years to find good, reliable sources. Here are some of the best, based on my years of research.

Suggested Books

The Jewish Hand in the World Wars, by Thomas Dalton; 2019; Castle Hill.

Eternal Strangers: Critical Views of Jews and Judaism Through the Ages, by Thomas Dalton; 2020; Castle Hill.

Germany's War, by John Wear; 2014; American Free Press.

Hitler's War, by David Irving; 1977; Viking.

Hitler's Revolution, by Richard Tedor; 2014; R. Tedor Publishing.

Mein Kampf, by Adolf Hitler (2 volumes), edited by Thomas Dalton; 2022; Clemens & Blair. (By far the best English translation.)

The Essential Mein Kampf, by Adolf Hitler, edited by Thomas Dalton; 2019; Clemens & Blair. (Contains the best passages from both volumes.)

Hitler on the Jews, by Adolf Hitler, edited by Thomas Dalton; 2019; Castle Hill.

Goebbels on the Jews, by Joseph Goebbels, edited by Thomas Dalton; 2019; Castle Hill.

Pan-Judah! Political Cartoons of Der Stürmer, 1925 to 1945, by Robert Penman, original drawings by Philipp 'Fips' Rupprecht; 2021; Clemens & Blair. (200 colorized and restored drawings, most of Jews.)

Pan-Judah! Volume Two, by Robert Penman, original drawings by Fips Rupprecht; 2022; Clemens & Blair. (200 more colorized cartoons.)

Unmasking Anne Frank, by Ikuo Suzuki; 2022; Clemens & Blair. (Best, and only, serious critique of the Anne Frank diary.)

The Holocaust: An Introduction, by Thomas Dalton; 2016; Castle Hill. (Best short critical study of the Holocaust.)

Debating the Holocaust: A New Look at Both Sides (4th ed.), by Thomas Dalton; 2020; Castle Hill. (Best overall book on the Holocaust; all aspects of the story are covered.)

Lectures on the Holocaust, by Germar Rudolf; 2011; Castle Hill. (An excellent, easily-readable look at the many Holocaust problems.)

The Gas Chamber of Sherlock Holmes, by Samuel Crowell; 2011; Nine-Banded Books. (Good, non-technical discussion of Holocaust issues.)

The Poisonous Mushroom, by Ernst Hiemer; 2020; color drawings by Fips Rupprecht; Clemens & Blair. (A classic children's book, showing the dangers of mixing with Jews.)

German Youth, Your Leader!, edited by Thomas Dalton; 2023; Clemens & Blair. (A book for youth and early teens, on Hitler's life; many colorized Fips images.)

Classic Essays on the Jewish Question: 1850 to 1945, edited by Thomas Dalton; 2022; Clemens & Blair. (16 classic essays critical of Jews and Jewish power.)

The Steep Climb, by Thomas Dalton; 2023; Clemens & Blair. (35 major essays by Dalton on Jews and the Jewish Question, revised and updated.)

Suggested Publishers and Websites

Clemens & Blair, LLC—publisher of high-quality books on Hitler, National Socialism, and the Jewish Question (www.clemensandblair.com).

Castle Hill Publishers—another top-notch producer of books, especially on the Holocaust (www.castlehillpublishers.com).

The Barnes Review—publisher of quality books on a variety of related topics (www.barnesreview.org).

Ostara Publications—leading British producer of books on these topics (www.ostarapublications.com).

Website of Thomas Dalton: www.thomasdaltonphd.com

Website of John Wear: www.wearswar.wordpress.com

The Occidental Observer: www.theoccidentalobserver.net

The Committee for Open Debate on the Holocaust: www.codoh.com

Suggested Videos

"Europa—The Last Battle"

"Adolf Hitler: The Greatest Story Never Told"

Triumph of the Truth 59

APPENDIX A
ASSORTED GRAPHICS and MEMES

THE MOST PRIVILEGED & WEALTHY GROUP OF PEOPLE ON EARTH ARE USING CENSORSHIP TO HIDE THEIR LIES & CRIMES FROM THE REST OF HUMANITY - THUS ROBBING ALL OTHERS OF THEIR FREEDOM

"The Forum should be seen as an exercise in the spread and influence of international Jewish power and activism. The number of representatives alone from various organizations totalled just over one thousand...

"...The 'recommendations' of the Forum include a demand to adopt "a clear industry standard for defining hate speech and anti-Semitism." This, of course, would be a definition of 'hate speech' and 'anti-Semitism' that would serve Jewish interests most effectively. This definition would be sufficiently wide-ranging that it would preclude, under threat of severe punishment, any criticism of Jews or Israel. This effort cannot be seen as isolated but as part of a conscious broader, global strategy."

from the article "Jews Continue Pressure for Internet Censorship" by Andrew Joyce, Ph.D.
Occidental Observer 19th of May 2015

THE JERUSALEM POST

Government anti-Semitism conference endorses net censorship

Recommendations coming out of the three day meeting included the scrubbing of Holocaust denial websites from the internet and the omission of "hate websites and content" from web searches.

By SAM SOKOL   Published: MAY 14, 2015 19:18

Leon Degrelle remembers Adolf Hitler

"After 1945 Hitler was accused of every cruelty, but it was not in his nature to be cruel. He loved children. It was an entirely natural thing for him to stop his car and share his food with young cyclists along the road. Once he gave his raincoat to a derelict plodding in the rain. At midnight he would interrupt his work and prepare the food for his dog Blondi"

"Anything that might have seemed too solemn in his remarks, he quickly tempered with a touch of humour… He could be harsh and even implacable in his judgments and yet almost at the same time be surprisingly conciliatory, sensitive and warm."

Quotes taken from "The enigma of Adolf Hitler" by Leon Degrelle

Jews have always wanted to live as a privileged class, divinely-chosen and beyond scrutiny. This attitude has made them unlikeable everywhere.

The Jewish race is therefore a unique case. Hitler had no intention of destroying it. He wanted the Jews to find their own identity in their own environment, but not to the detriment of others. The fight - if we can call it that - of National Socialism against the Jews was purely limited to one objective: that the Jews leave Germany in peace. It was planned to give them a country of their own, outside Germany. Madagascar was contemplated, but the plans were dropped when the United States entered the war. In the meanwhile, Hitler thought of letting the Jews live in their own traditional ghettos. They would have their own administration, they would run their own affairs, and would live as they wanted. They had their own police, their own tramways, their own flag, and their own businesses.

from The Story of the Waffen SS essay by Leon Degrelle

'You can easily understand how that within a few years Hitler will emerge from the hatred that surrounds him now as one of the most significant figures who ever lived,' ...

'He had in him the stuff of which legends are made.'

John F. Kennedy
Diary Entry
1945

Social Renaissance

"Germany's triumph over unemployment, without foreign help and during worldwide economic depression, was in itself an accomplishment any government could be satisfied with. For Hitler, it was a step toward far-reaching social programs intended to elevate and unify the population…

"Hitler believed that removing traditional class barriers would create social mobility for talented individuals to advance. All Germany would benefit through the maturation of the more promising human resources."

from "Hitler's Revolution"
by Richard Tedor
Published 2014

APPENDIX B
ORIGINAL CARTOONS by ROBERT PENMAN

Triumph of the Truth

Triumph of the Truth

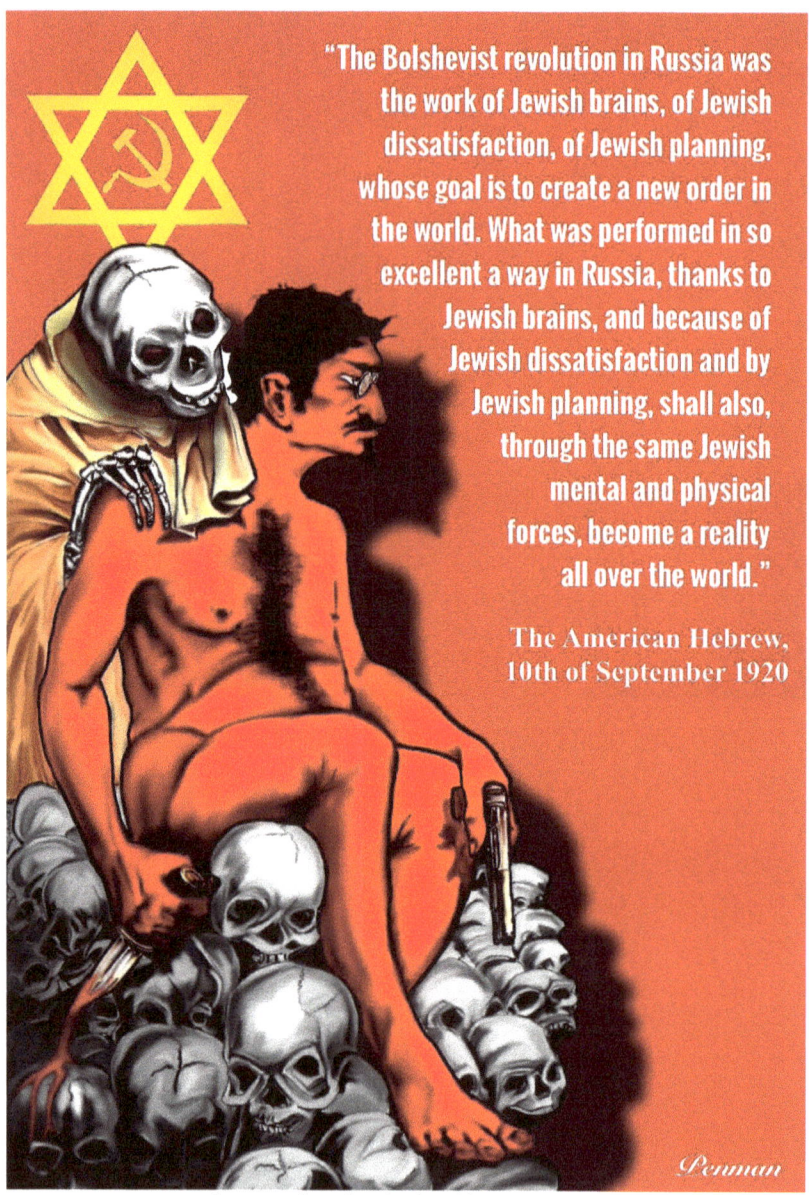

(restored and colorized by Penman)

ENDNOTES

[1] Cited in *Russia from the American Embassy* (1921), p. 214.
[2] US government archives, telegram 02a.
[3] Article titled "Jews in world reconstruction" by S. Tonjoroff; pages 434 and 507.
[4] Sources: (1): Sever Plocker, "Stalin's Jews," www.ynetnews.com, 12-21-06; (2): "About 40 percent of high-ranking NKVD officers had Jewish nationality recorded in their identity documents," writes Yale University professor Timothy Snyder in *Bloodlands: Europe Between Hitler and Stalin*, "as did more than half of the NKVD generals. . . . The Great Terror could be, and by many would be, blamed on the Jews." (3): "Robert Wilton, though, reported that in 1918 the Central Committee of the Bolshevik party had twelve members, of whom nine [75%] were of Jewish origin and three were of Russian ancestry. R. Wilton, *The Last Days of the Romanovs* (IHR, 1993), p. 185; (4): H. Greife, *Slave Labor in Soviet Russia* (1937); (5): George Simons, "Bolshevik Propaganda": Hearings before a subcommittee of the Committee on the Judiciary, US Senate (1919): "in the northern community of Petrograd…out of 388 members, only 16 happened to be real Russians, and all the rest Jews…" [thus, 372/388 = 96% Jewish], pp. 114-115.
[5] *You, Gentiles* (1924), p. 155.
[6] "The role of Jews in the Russian revolutionary movement." *The Slavonic and East European Review*, vol 40, no 94 (1961), pp. 164-165.
[7] *The Jews of the Soviet Union* (1990), p. 86.
[8] "Reply to an Inquiry of the Jewish News Agency in the United States," 12 Jan 1931.
[9] *The Jewish State* (1869/1967), p. 26.
[10] The full Protocols can be found, for example, at www.islam-radio.net.
[11] For details, see *The Jewish Hand in the World Wars*, by T. Dalton (2019), pp. 39-50.
[12] From *Mein Kampf* (T. Dalton, ed.), 2022, pp. 219-221.
[13] From his article "A real case against the Jews" (1928), reprinted in *Classic Essays on the Jewish Question* (2022), T. Dalton, ed.
[14] *Daily Express* (24 Mar 1933).
[15] Cited in *The Bloody Red Streak,* by T. David (1951).
[16] Cited in *Storm on the Horizon* (2000), by J. Doenecke, p. 440.
[17] Cited in *The White House Papers of Harry Hopkins* (1948; vol 1), by R. Sherwood, p. 111.
[18] Cited in *The Patriarch*, by D. Nasaw (2012), pp. 357-358.
[19] Cited in *The Jewish Hand in the World Wars*, by T. Dalton (2019), p. 110.
[20] Cited in ibid. (p. 111).
[21] Cited in ibid. (p. 118).
[22] Cited in *The Secret Diary of Harold Ickes* (1954), by H. Ickes, p. 676.
[23] JTA.org, 6 Sep 1939, "Chamberlain welcomes Agency's war aid."

[24] "The Leuchter Report," by Fred Leuchter, *Journal of Historical Review* (1989), 9(2).
[25] *Germany's War* (2014), by J. Wear, p. 383.
[26] *The Gas Chamber of Sherlock Holmes* (2011), by S. Crowell, pp. 58, 93.
[27] See the books by Thomas Dalton: *The Holocaust: An Introduction* (2016) or *Debating the Holocaust* (2020, 4th ed.).
[28] Cited in *Allied Wartime Diplomacy* (1958), by E. Rozek, pp. 209-210. Letter dated 29 Feb 1944.
[29] "The battle for Berlin in World War Two," BBC.co.uk, 3-10-11.
[30] Cited in *Nemesis at Potsdam* (1979), by A. de Zayas.
[31] See Delmer: *Trail Sinister* (1961) and *Black Boomerang* (1962).
[32] From Grimm's book *Political Justice*. Cited by U. Walendy, *The Methods of Reeducation* (1979).
[33] For all these passages, see *Goebbels on the Jews* (2019), by T. Dalton.
[34] See *Eternal Strangers* (2020), by T. Dalton.

www.ingramcontent.com/pod-product-compliance
Lightning Source LLC
LaVergne TN
LVHW061625070526
838199LV00070B/6589